£6.95

Hoffnung's
MUSICAL CHAIRS

Books by

GERARD HOFFNUNG

Hoffnung's The Maestro
The Hoffnung Symphony Orchestra
The Hoffnung Music Festival
The Hoffnung Companion to Music
Hoffnung's Musical Chairs
Hoffnung's Acoustics

Hoffnung's

Musical Chairs

GERARD HOFFNUNG

LONDON 2000

First published 1958
jointly by Dennis Dobson Ltd
and Putnam & Co Ltd

2nd impression April 1959
3rd impression August 1960
4th impression October 1962
5th impression September 1965
6th impression December 1968
7th impression December 1972
8th impression October 1975
9th impression May 1978
10th impression May 1978 (Paperback)
and subsequently re-published by
Souvenir Press from 1983

This edition published by
The Hoffnung Partnership
44 Pilgrims Lane
London NW3 1SN

ISBN 1 903643 04 X

Cover and book design
Vera Brice and Leslie Robinson

Printed and bound in Great Britain
by St Edmundsbury Press
Blenheim Industrial Park, Newmarket Road
Bury St Edmunds, Suffolk, IP33 3TU

For
MALCOLM ARNOLD

Acknowledgements

Grateful thanks are due to Ian Hislop for his contribution to this book, and also to its designers and printers for the infinite care and consideration they have taken in its production.

Foreword

As a child I loved the musical drawings of Gerard Hoffnung because they made the serious-looking world of classical music seem funny and accessible. As an adult I like them even more and find the cartoons intelligent, witty, absurd, surreal and all the other adjectives that adults use when they mean that they still find things funny. But Hoffnung's work remains timeless delight because his world is so innocent. I do not mean by this that the drawings are sentimental or naïve. On the contrary, they are sophisticated and beautifully observed but the tone of the drawing is one of engaged affection for the musical life and all its foibles. This little collection, the perfect gift to slip in the pocket of any concert-goer, shows Hoffnung's gift for transforming the instruments of the orchestra into a variety of animals or household objects. My own favourite is the famous drawing of the cat who is playing his own whiskers with a bow operated by his tail. Typically for the artist this one joke is not enough, so that the whiskers become not just the strings of the instrument but also the stave on which the notes are written. The tradition of the cartooning seems recognisably German, the whimsy seems unmistakably English but in the end I suspect the appeal of the drawings is actually universal.

Ian Hislop

Carnival of Animals

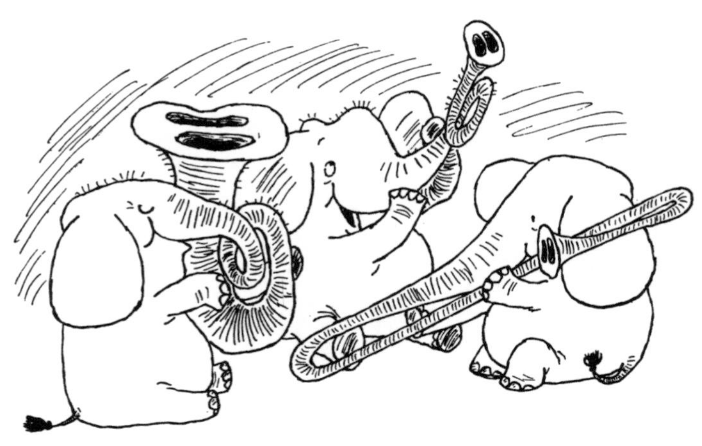

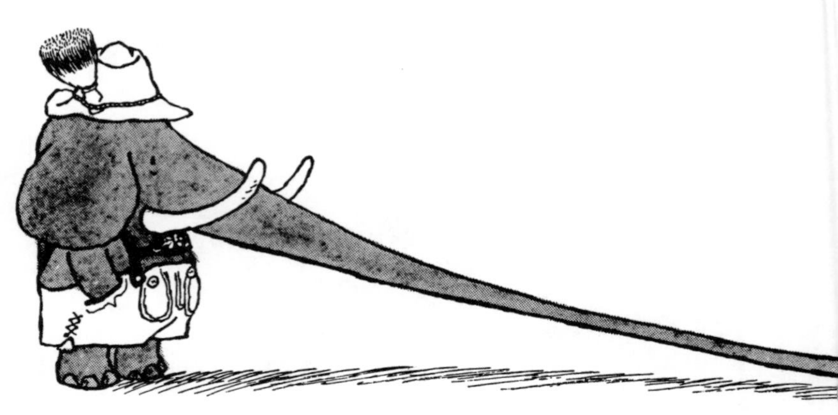

G.H.

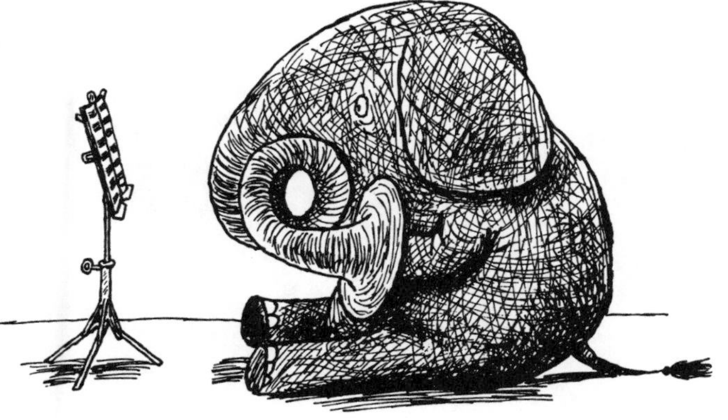

Bechstein

Hoffnung

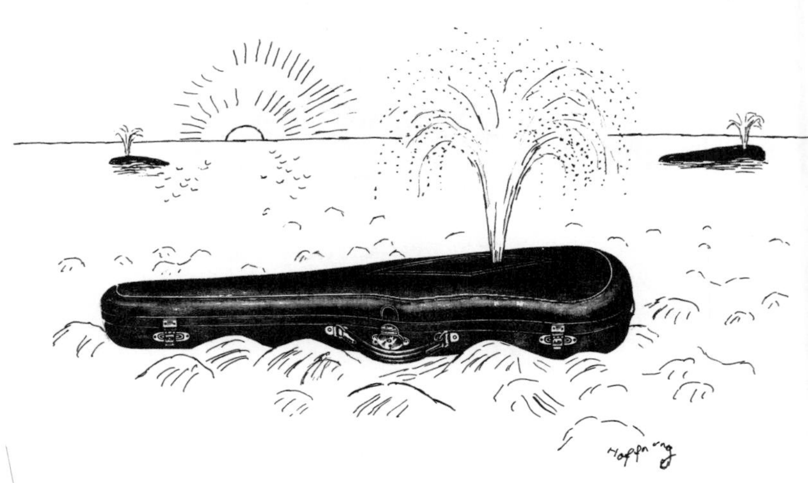

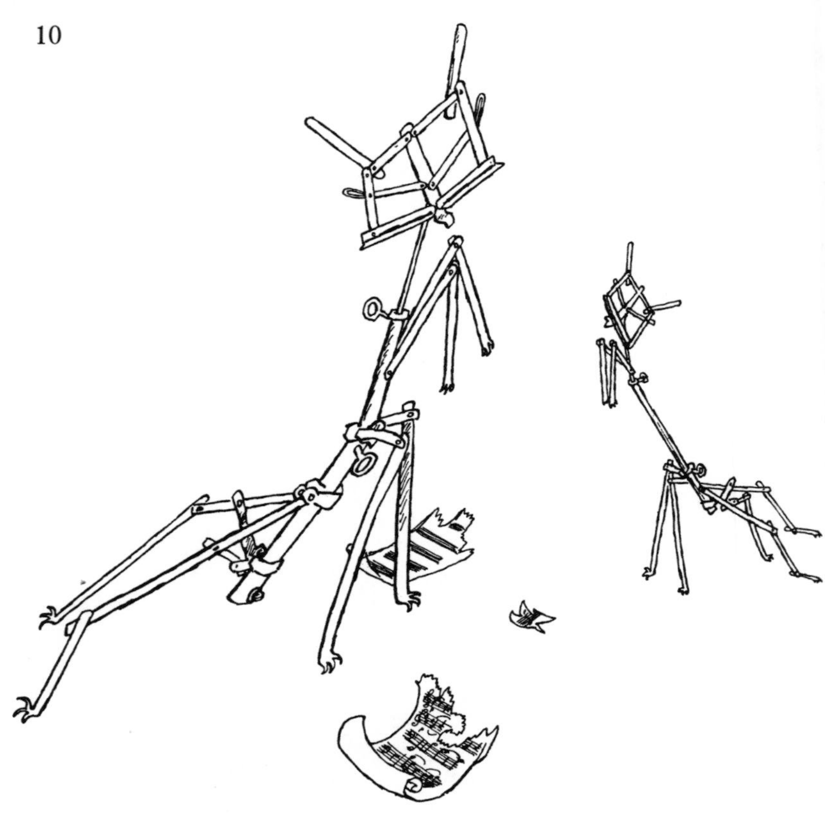

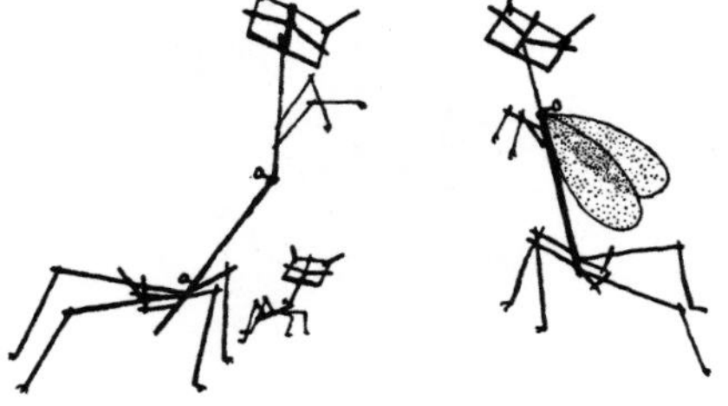

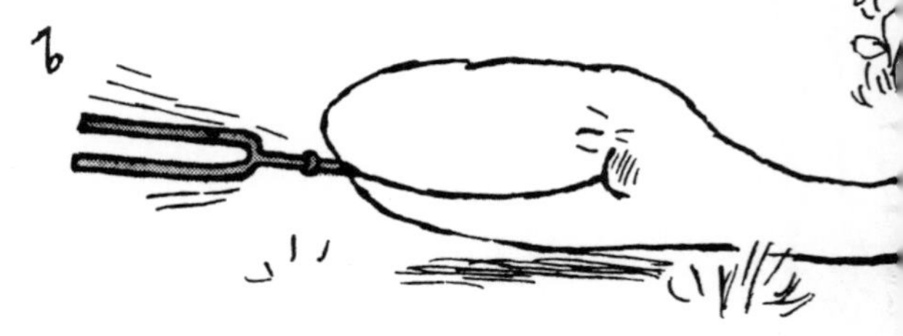

Light Cavalry

Early outbreaks of Rock 'n Roll

Rites of Spring

C
D
E
F
G
A
H
C
D
H.

Mountain horn (in E flat)

A Chapel in the Valley

lies
musician.
Hoffnung

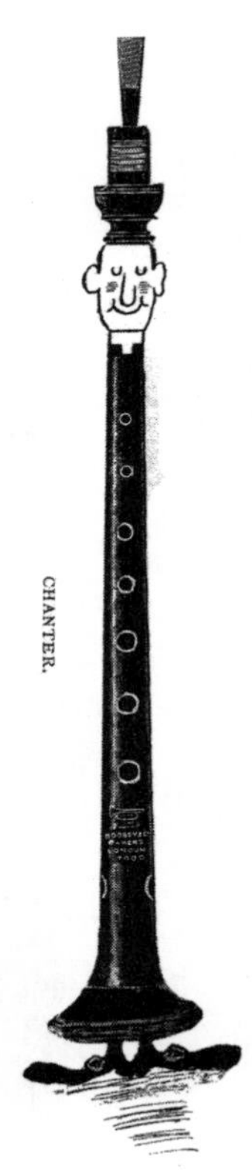

CHANTER.

H.

Marche Funèbre

Symphonia Domestica

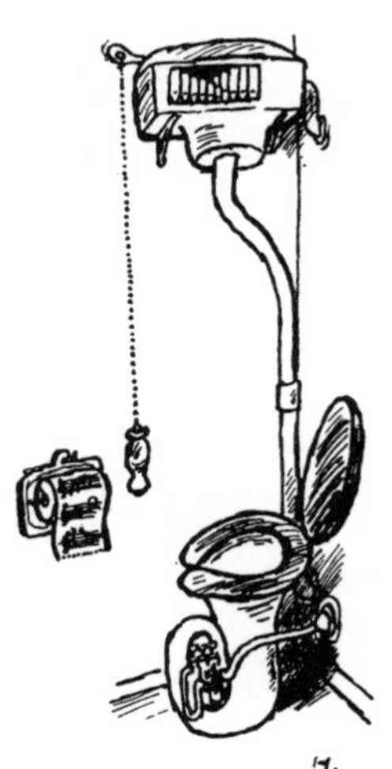

"Did you ring, Sir?"

HOFFNUNG

Children's Corner

Impromptu à la mode

The Trumpet Shall Sound

Allegro con spirito

Calm Sea and a Prosperous Voyage

Postlude

3.

4.

5.
6.

7.

8.

THE END.